# The No Nonsense Guide to Personal Branding for Career Success

*101 Practical Tips & Lessons*

Enjoy Business Series®

Bernard Kelvin Clive

# Praise for the Book

*"With the speed of changes in the world today, success has no geographical borders. In this engaging book, Bernard Kelvin Clive shares principles from his own success in Ghana that can inspire and guide readers anywhere in the world. With a gentle and humble spirit, he reminds us that building a name for ourselves is most easily done not by manipulating and pushing but simply by serving others. I highly recommend 'The No Nonsense Guide to Personal Branding' for anyone who has a voice to be heard."*

**Dan Miller, author of New York Times bestselling 48 Days to the Work You Love.**

*"BKC holds the power to transform a generation that seems lost in chaotic branding. Through his writings and motivation, he is able to command a power that motivates a change for the best. In the book, 'The No Nonsense Guide to Personal Branding for Career Success", BKC gives us the power to create appealing personal brands that sell our qualities to a target audience. I have greatly benefitted from this book, and will entreat educational institutions, corporates and any person/s that choose to live a full, purpose-filled life to connect to this guide"* ~ **Penelope S. Bartels-Sam, CEO, InCharge Global, a Celebrated Woman in Technology in Africa**

*"Bernard Kelvin Clive has done it again. He is a powerhouse in the art of personal branding and success. Clive takes a very difficult subject, personal branding, and*

*breaks it down into the fundamentals. We get the ABC's of success with this book. There is so much information contained in this book that he should be charging seminar fees just to have access to the book.*

*Clive doesn't try to sell you a magic pill for success. What he does do well is give you the insights necessary so that through hard work you can map your way to the top. I coach people every day on the steps and importance of personal branding, and I learned a few new things. This book isn't just for beginners, entrepreneurs at all levels can find what they are looking for in this book."* ~ **Allan Dubon, Author, Speaker. Social Media Coach, USA**

Clive not only guides us through the mapping of our success, but also provides us with resources and tools that will help us along the way. This is a must read, no matter where you find yourself on the personal branding ladder!

*"The Book provides the reader with a complete and concise methodology for establishing a brand in today's marketplace. Clive's writing style is easy and appealing and he engages the reader with thought-provoking questions. If you have never ever sold anything in the digital market and want to establish your presence and credibility, then this would be a great book to start with. I like the fact that he also addresses the concept of serving and giving back to your communities as well. This is a great addition to the digital marketers' library."* **~Michelle M. White, USA**

*"This book is an excellent addition to the other books written by Bernard Kelvin Clive. The internet, especially social media, makes it even easier to put our jobs and products out on the international globe dashboard in order to get to the masses. Some people are excelling in that aspect because of good branding; the least said about others the better. The internet opens doors to learn and form friendship (excerpts from the book). In this book, Bernard categorically outlines the reason why Businesses and individuals need to build strong and formidable brands that will not just last but help that career grow successfully. I recommend this book to Business Executives, Entrepreneurs, Students, just to mention but a few. Clive is a living testimony to Good Personal Branding. He is sharing that with us now, receive it freely."* ~ **Nana Ama Yeboah Diamond, C.E.O, Sangy Nursing Services, Speaker, Debate Arena (Facebook)**

*"This is one of the few books that teach how to build a personal brand through new media (social media). He shares the practical steps in using social media and other offline structures to build a personal brand. I recommend this to all the youth who love new media and are ready to create their own selling brand."* ~ **Kofi Yeboah, Blogger & Social Media Manager, IQ4News.**

*"I'm quite intrigued; in fact very much startled about the manner in which the author intelligently presented these ideas. They are simple, practical, realistic and yet very powerful principles that will be profitable to anyone seeking*

*to create a brand for himself no matter who he is or where he comes from"* ~ **Bismark Seth Opoku (University of Ghana. Legon)**

*"Branding You - made easier at last! Bernard Kelvin Clive has always served our generation with materials rich in transformational content; if adopted and worked with, Change with great results come to stay. With "The No Nonsense Guide to Personal Branding for Career Success" – another timely relevant piece, Bernard shares vital tips & instructions on excelling with very little or no stress using online and offline tools at our disposal, don't be left out! Read it and Succeed"* ~ **Cecil Ato Kwamena Dadzie (Ghanabakwamena), Volunteer, Youth Advocate, Blogger & Digital Communications Professional, Development Journalist & Co-Founder Instant Media Ghana.**

*"The words springing out of every line and page rings the sort of truth and motivation which is hard to ignore. If after reading this book, you continue living in no man's land...well fill in the blanks. Excellent job BKC!"* ~ **Linda Naa Oyoo Quartey, Blogger and Fashion Entrepreneur, Best Lifestyle Blogger 2013 (Ghana)**

*"The No Nonsense Guide to Personal Branding for Career Success", is about raising the bar, and setting yourself up as a yardstick of quality. It enlightens you on how to project self confidence in today's fast paced world. Bernard Kelvin Clive takes a calculated approach to dissect the critical issues pertaining to pre and post personal brand*

*development principles that resonates with the "newbie", the intermediate, and the professional, who all have the common desire to simply be winners in their chosen endeavors"* ~ **Daniel Boakye, Web Programmer Alexandria -VA - USA**

**Thanks for purchasing this book; this is your FREE Gift**

www.BKC.name/GIFT

## Copyright© 2013 Bernard Kelvin Clive

ISBN-13: 978-1492973393

ISBN-10: 1492973394

For permission requests, please contact the Publisher or the Author.

www.BKC.name

Tel: +233244961121

# Books by the same author

1. *The Art of Personal Branding*

2. *Your Dreams Will Not Die*

3. *Inspirational Kitchen – Discover 30 Ingredients to Spice up your Life*

4. *Just A Minute – 52 Seconds: Simplified Motivation – Words to Inspire*

5. *The Writers' Dream: How to Write, Publish and Sell your Book Successfully(Paper Back)*

6. *16 secrets I Learnt From My EX*

7. *How to Publish and Sell your Books with Little or No Money*

8. *Do Not Die with your Music Unsung*

9. *EnjoyLife 360*

10. *How To DO It At Any Age*

11. *The No Nonsense Guide to Effective Time Management: 187 Little Tips that Create Big Impact*

Dedicated to YOU!

# Acknowledgements

I'm very grateful to the Almighty God for life, health, wealth and the wisdom given to me to inspire generations to live their God-given dreams. To my dear family, Mum, Elizabeth Janis Amoako, Dad, Nana Akora-Ampem II, Twin Sister, Bernice Marfo(Mrs). Hey! You Maame Acey Yamaoh(Beatrice), Ebenezer Addo thanks for your encouragements.

Bright Dela Dey, Seth Boss Kay and Romeo Adzah Dowokpor, you guys rock; you took time to read, edit and offer suggestions to make this book happen!
Isaac Ieboah of DreamHub thanks for the great cover design. Ebenezer Addo-Mensah Saka of Saka Homes, I truly appreciate your support.
Selorm Alfred Betepe of Selort Group, and all the team members, God bless you.

## Table of Contents

# What you will find

In this guide, I share with you the system that other successful people and me have used and still use to help  you position your #Brand and #Business, to reach unimaginable heights.

It's time to build your personal brand and career.

**#MyStory -** I am a firm believer that this era holds more promise for businesses and individuals than ever before. Though I wasn't born into the age of social media, I quickly adapted to it. Way back in 1999—back when the Y2K scare was growing and having an email address made you a hero—I used a desktop computer to access the World Wide Web for the first time. You can only imagine how excited I was to tap into this new technology. I considered going to an internet cafe a luxury. Chatting on Yahoo messenger was as much of a joy as Facebook and Whatsapp are today.

I joined an active online community (48days.net by Dan Miller) in 2010, a time when I was busy writing my first book "Your Dreams Will Not Die." Being a part of that community allowed me to gain a lot of insight about blogging, writing and creating podcasts.

In 2010, I began podcasting. I used my Dell laptop with its inbuilt microphone to record minute-long motivational messages. At first, my podcast wasn't very well known. In those days only few pastors delivered their sermons via podcast. Aside these few, no one else in Ghana was doing it. Still, I persisted. I later began recording some of the podcasts from a professional studio, and also got a high-quality headset to use with my laptop. I experimented with different podcast platforms. I began gaining subscribers, and at one point I had over 50,000 downloads. Soon, I got my podcast ranked #1 on iTunes Ghana and Botswana under the Self-Help category.

In addition to producing a successful podcast, I have successfully published close to a dozen books (two of which have been translated to French, a first for any Ghanaian motivational author) which are all available on <u>Amazon</u>. Three of my books have also been converted to audiobooks, a move I made when I saw a complete lack of Ghanaian audiobooks on the market. I am also the first Ghanaian author to have his book converted into a mobile app (Inspiration Kitchen 101, available for free on Google Play). In addition, I am proud to be the first resident Ghanaian author to have a book that is an Amazon Bestseller.

In 2012, I was honoured to deliver the commencement speech for the College of Art & Social Sciences at the Kwame Nkrumah University of Science & Technology, Ghana.

I say all of this not to boast, but to inspire you to do even more in your life. With commitment, hard work, persistence, and prayer, anything is possible. The advancement of technology makes this all the more true. The internet opens new doors to learn, to form friendships, and to travel the length and breadth of the world, touching many hearts along the way.

By no means will I say I have arrived. I'm still traveling this road, practicing and polishing my skills and knowledge as I go.

Finally, just as proof that my system works, Google "Inspirational speakers in Ghana" or "public speakers in Ghana" to see the very first result that Google returns. Enjoy the read.

# Introduction

Having an impressive business card, profile, resume or CV is not enough anymore to land you your next job or gig. You will need a strong personal brand.

Social media has become an integral part of our lives in this age. More companies are relying on social media for job recruitment and many job seekers are also using the same medium to get jobs. How then do you as a person, professionally brand and position yourself to be a likely candidate for your next job, to be picked by your employee? How do you stand out from the masses, how do you become the preferred choice?

This simple guide is an attempt to provide basic practical tips to help you:

Whether you are looking for a job or selling something or recruiting, this will help you. It's either you brand yourself or are branded out. The time is now!

When I talk about personal branding for social change and service, with the focus on people who passionately pursue their cause for the higher benefits of humanity, I am talking about the likes of Madam Theresa who sacrificed her life to serve the poor in the village of Calcutta; she didn't make a name for herself. Vincent Van Gogh, a great painter, painted his heart out in every little work he did not to make masterpieces but today every piece of his works is celebrated as a masterpiece. Nelson Mandela, chose peace for his country instead, not pride, selfish ambitions or revenge after all he had suffered. The bottom line is this: personal branding is not about personal bragging, positions, status, making a name; it's about service, impact, what you bring to the market place, meeting the needs of others. Your value, gifts will make room and name for you. **Let's serve**.

### *A Quick Overview*

The governing values for this book on personal branding are built around these four keys: 4D's and 4P's.

Here they are:

- ✓ **Discovery** – *Personal Discovery* ~ **Purpose.**
- ✓ **Development –** *Working on your talents* ~ **Preparation.**
- ✓ **Design** – *Platform building, Career and work life* ~ **Positioning**

✓ **Deployment** – *Service and execution* ~ **Publicity**, Promotion

You can always evaluate yourself with these keys on your personal branding and career journey; it's an ongoing cycle and not one-off act.

## #PepTalk

Hear this... Sometimes I have folks telling me that someone is already doing what they intended doing and the market is saturated; lots of brand names and that almost everyone is selling the same product and services. There could be some truth in that though, but understand that *we live in the world of abundance.*

Hear me now on this, whatever you desire to do, you will certainly find a trace of it somewhere, but if you truly believe that's what you are called to do and you are passionate about it and you believe in that cause, *__do it__*!

---

*"If a man is called to be a street sweeper, he should sweep streets even as Michelangelo painted, or Beethoven composed music, or Shakespeare wrote poetry. He should sweep streets so well that all the hosts of heaven and earth will pause to say, here lived a great street sweeper who did his job well" ~ Martin Luther King Jr.*

Let me give you some examples: No matter the platforms and crusades Bill Graham will have, he can never win/convert every sinner; no matter how much Les Brown motivates, he can't inspire every soul; no matter how many albums or downloads Lady Gaga, Sarkodie and Kirk Franklin get for their music, they will never appeal to everyone. The 'Harry Porter' movie and book series don't appeal to everyone nor meet their expectations. All the above mentioned names have great brand names and fame.

This is the point, there are certain people who will never be educated, unless you teach them, others will not be saved unless you speak to them, some souls will never be motivated unless you speak, and someone will never know joy or fun unless you sing. I mean you reading this now. Everyone has been called to meet the need of others in special ways, however big or small. It may not be large crowds and big acts but tiny little acts.

---

*"When you do the common things in life in an uncommon way, you will command the attention of the world." - George Washington Carve*

Today don't give up because someone else is doing it or even doing better than you can, don't let go because you are not on TV and don't have that fame and publicity the others are enjoying, you are uniquely unique, your service counts, you count. Heaven is counting on you today. Smile and get to work. Sing that song, write that book, share that gift, say that prayer, *Do it*! God bless you**!**

If you have not yet read my Book

## *"The Art of Personal Branding"*

Do get it now! It has tons of practical information.

## Demystifying Personal Branding

1. Personal branding is not about popularity, fame and self-promotion. It's about service and value to others. Do your name, product and service affect others positively? Think value creation. #ProblemSolving

2. Personal Branding is not about having a fancy business card, waving and distributing it everywhere you go. Design is only a little part of the brand identity. You don't spend all your energy on that. Get your focus right. Let's come home; I believe everyone knows at least one exceptional "Waakye" and "Koko" seller in your hood that almost everyone wants to buy from though there are other sellers. She has neither a business card nor even a name for her shop, just a ghetto but she provides an incredible service. That's it! Focus and the main thing, invaluable service delivery. #differentiation

3. Personal branding is not about personal bragging; spreading your accolades and credentials all over the place. Trying all you can to be at the very top to be noticed. Driven by selfish ambitions, your thought becomes - me, me, and me! Think about the other person. How can people benefit from all

that you have learnt and acquired? If it has no meaning to others then it becomes vanity. #Significance

4. Personal Branding is not about the number of fans and followers you have on social media. It's about being social, positively influencing the lives of others. People are seeking connection and communication not to be commanded and controlled. It's about #purpose, passion, preparation, provision.

*NOTE: When I talk about personal branding, I'm not talking about gaming the system, tips and tricks to go viral or becoming the next hit Gangman Style video. I talk about genuine service; providing value and building trust.*

# Reasons Why You Need Personal Branding for your Career

---

*Tom Peters rightly said "All of us need to understand the importance of branding. We are CEOs of our own companies: Me Inc. To be in business today, our most important job is to be head marketer for the brand called You."*

Let me share this story with you from the good old book. The story is told of the seven sons of Sceva[Acts 19:13-20]. His sons saw Paul casting out demons and they thought they could do likewise. However, when they tried it on a demon possessed man, they had the beating of their lives. The demon squeezed the juice out of them, LOL! Like a commercial that reads *"don't try this at home"*. Now, if you are familiar with the story or not you might have not thought about it this way... This is what happens to most individuals/brands (personal brands). When they observe others starting and succeeding in any venture, they quickly copy and jump into it; now every young dude wants to 'be his/her own boss'. Most people are just hopping onto the social media frenzy. And with the Oil discovery in Ghana, you will find most companies & individuals having 'Oil & Gas' services as part of their business model, interesting huh! Another typical local example (when a neighbour starts a 'provision shop', within days there will be chains of shops around. If you do remember when the "pure water" and "space to space" business began, it shortly caught on like uncontrolled wild fire). [*All these have their advantages when put in the right perspective*]. This keeps happening time and time again - the copycats are everywhere. But time will prove the authentic ones. Major question to answer is '*Why do you do what you do?* From the story, the sons of Sceva lacked these attributes in the area of personal branding:

I.      They had no foundation: brands are built on the foundation of purpose and trust.

II.     They had no credibility (the demon said, 'Paul we know, Jesus we know, but who are you?') that's it. Who are you? What do you have to prove that you are capable of doing the same work? You must be trustworthy. Build a portfolio of works to serve as your reference point. Don't copy blindly.

III.    They lacked authority, power. Great brands have authority in the things they do, they provide value, they have proven track record, when they talk, others listen. They have influence. You got to invest time and energy into your chosen field and master the craft to have control and command. It earns you respect and great reputation. This will make you a 'go to' person. NB: strong brands are built overtime, not by shortcuts and copycats.

IV.    They did it for the wrong reason. They were seeking applause instead of doing it for a worthy cause. Personal Branding is not about imitation, it's about originality, authenticity & authority.

### So this is it:

1. People do business with those they trust, know and love. *So why not become such a person?*
2. Your brand proves your authority: that you are an expert in your field to be trusted.
3. Your personal brand becomes your business marketing channel to reach out to your market, your fans, your tribe, etc. That is your platform.
4. It boosts your confidence
5. It helps propel your career into unimaginable heights
6. It helps you distinguish yourself from the masses
7. It provides more visibility, exposure and breakthroughs
8. It helps you to land your next job or gig with ease

9. It enables you to understand yourself better and utilize your strengths
10. It leads in sales increase of your product and services
11. It provides you with the ability to find your target market with ease and also positions you to be found.
12. It increases your market value, your worth. Positioning you a as an expert
13. You will be perceived as more credible

> *"It's important to build a personal brand because it's the only thing you're going to have. Your reputation online, and in the new business world is pretty much the game, so you've got to be a good person. You can't hide anything, and more importantly, you've got to be out there at some level."* -

Gary Vaynerchuk, Author of Crush it!

## Building your #PersonalBrand the F.A.S.T. way

**F~ Find** your true voice, and fine tune it. What makes you unique and how uniquely can you do an ordinary task? Don't imitate, it irritates. Be original.

**A~ Add** value to others and what you do. Ask yourself, how can I make this more meaningful to others? What can I bring to the market place to meet a need? To solve a problem, to enhance an existing system, product or service? Think value!

**S~ Stay** true to your goal, which are true to your chosen path. Be true to your values, your customers. You got to be consistent. Keep at it.

**T~ Trust**; build trust. You must be trustworthy. Can you be trusted, will you stay true to your promise of delivery. Note: trust is the new currency for riches in this age. Be credible.

We are in an age where personal branding matters, build yours the FAST way.

**Note:** It takes time to build great brands.

**It's time to get the real work done. Let's go!**

## Let's get started:

*"When you are inspired by some great purpose, some extraordinary project, all your thoughts break their bounds. Your mind transcends limitations, your consciousness expands in every direction and you find yourself in a new, great and wonderful world. Dormant forces, faculties and talents become alive, and you discover yourself to be a greater person by far than you ever dreamed yourself to be." ~ Patanjali*

It's important to note that getting a job or pursuing a career is more than just money; it's about your life, your future, purpose and fulfillment. So it's time to think through your decisions and options before taking the next step.

## Your Career

*"Find out what you like doing best and get someone to pay you for doing it." –Katherine Whitehorn*

Let's get the definition of a career to help us along the way:

Career is defined by the Oxford English Dictionary as a person's "course or progress through life (or a distinct portion of life)". In this definition, career is understood to relate to a range of aspects of an individual's life, learning and work. Career is also frequently understood to relate only to the working aspects of an individual's life e.g. as in career woman. A third way in which the term career is used, is to describe an occupation or a profession that usually involves special training or formal education,[1] and is considered to be a person's lifework.[2] In this case "a career" is seen as a sequence of related jobs usually pursued within a single industry or sector e.g. "a career in law" or "a career in the building trade".

The etymology of the term comes from the French word carriere (16 c.) ("road, racecourse") which, in turn, comes from the <u>Latin</u> word "(via) cararia" (track for wheeled vehicles) which originated from the Latin word *carrus" which means "wagon".* ~Source <u>Wikipedia</u>

Let's take a look at the word "Career" We can break it into 'Care' and 'er'[Excellence Reward. This is how I define career from those two words; it's something you 'care' about passionately, that you execute with excellence and reward you eventually. So if you do what you love with excellence, its rewards will come in terms of riches and fulfillment. That should be your ultimate goal: *Service in love with excellence and distinction.*

Your career journey is not one straight route uphill, it will be filled with ups and downs and learning curves along the way; be flexible and ready to adjust.

#Tip: *It's imperative to have a career coach.*

**Note**: One secret about people who made it to the top of their careers and are celebrated in their chosen fields is that they chose careers based on their gifts and talents. Additionally, they most often have the testimony that someone believed in them. Someone saw what they could become than what there were then. That didn't end there, they helped develop and nurture those skills and abilities in them. It's always best to find someone who believes in you, your product and services. A person who will not give up on you till your star begins to shine and the greatness in you shows. On the other hand, if you have not yet found anyone who believes in you, keep working at improving yourself daily. Bettering yourself, you will eventually be discovered and even if it doesn't happen, you will become an expert in your chosen field.

*"A successful brand is always built on the foundation of passion and purpose"*

## A successful career life always begins with you.

*"The simple truth is that if we stop trying to "fix" our employees and rather focus on their strengths and their passions, we can create a fervent army of brand evangelists who, when empowered, could take our brand and our products to a whole new level."* ~Forbes.com

### ✓ Knowing yourself: Purpose: why you do what you do?

Let me share this story with you from the SeattleTimes, A college fraternity invited a favorite professor for an evening meal and then a discussion. During the discussion, the professor turned to the student and asked, "What are you living for, young man?"" The student replied, "I am going to be an electrical engineer." "Yes," replied the professor, "I understand that's going to be your profession but what are you living for?" The young man was thoughtful and apparently baffled by the question. Finally he said, "I am sorry, sir, but I guess I haven't thought that one through."

That's my question for you today as well... What are you living for? You should be able to answer this question clearly, because that will be your foundation for building your career and brand on.

*"Self-discovery is the key to success and excellence in life."*

**Purpose**: is the reason for which something was created. Everyone has a purpose and nobody showed up on earth by an accident. Simply to find ones purpose you need to seek the Grand Of Designers (GOD Almighty).

Let's take the acronym **PURPOSE** as a guiding path

**P** – Passion, find what you are truly passionate about.

**U** – Understand yourself. "Man Know thyself" Identify your strengths and weakness.

**R** – Resources, find out the tools and materials that can help sharpen your gifts; polish your craft.

**P** – Positioning; Personal Branding, this is what sets you apart from the others.

**O** – Opportunities – your gift will make room for you. If you don't find opportunities, create them.

**S** – Serve, we are called to service. Your purpose is embodied in contributing to the total wellbeing of others.

**E** – Earn, if you do all these well, you will earn trust, credibility, good reputation, money and you will enjoy life and a sense of satisfaction in pursuing your dreams.

- Start the journey of self-discovery, self-awareness, self-reliance, deep thinking, reflection, prayers, listening and drawing from your talents. It's very necessary to take self-assessment tests to aid you in this journey. Ensure you do your SWOT analysis [Strengths – Weaknesses – Opportunities – Threats].
- Your personal values: what is important to you? List your five core values. And be prepared to make adjustment to your current state of life.

*For further reading on the subject of purpose and career, I will recommend the book "**48 Days to the Work You Love**" by Dan Miller*

*"Use what talents you possess: the woods would be very silent if no birds sang there except those that sang best" ~Henry Van Dyke*

## You will need:

i.  Personal mission statement: inculcating your purpose, goal, dreams and career paths together. This will be your map, your future to success.

ii.      Career paths: goals & ambitions, choice of work, work pattern and life style.

iii.     A career plan. Your strategy for success. Combining your purpose, values, career goals all into action plan. How to find that job you want, or create the career you desire, or be posited to be more employable or to find or be found by your employer.

*Answer these questions?*

- How do I prepare myself for my next job career?
- Are my current skills the right skill-set required for the job I'm looking for?
- Is my current location best to be located by my employer?
- Can I be found if they are searching for a person with all the skills, qualities and experience I have?

*Whether you find or you are found, you must be proactive.*

i.      **How to find?** Here you are going on a hunt, looking for your next employer, your next client, your next gig, your next deal. You must know where your clients or employers' searching for people with the qualities you have are located. Where do people searching for the product and services you have hangout out? What are their communication channels, online or phone? Their location, demographics.

You must clearly outline all these. NB*: You don't go to Europe in winter to sell Ice creams.* Knowing all these, you need some tools to enhance your search. You learn how to use search tools, such as Google, using tweet search with hash tags, Facebook graph search, etc. using online communities, forums and blogs.

ii. **How to be found?** The worse situation to be in is having the best of products, services and be better qualified for a job position but can't be found. Nobody knows you and what you can offer. To be found online here are some things to do:

- Profiling (we *will talk more about this later in the book*)
- Get a website, blog, online portfolio; that could be your greatest asset for your brand.
- Have your website/blog optimized for SEO.
- Join an online community of like-minded people.
- Join social network sites and actively participate, Facebook, Twitter, Tumblr, LinkedIn, etc.
- Attend online webinars and ask questions

Offline: attend workshops, networking events; events where you can potentially be located by your prospective client or employer. Interact with others, ask for recommendations and referrals.

**Now let's delve into this…#brand building**

## A to Z Simple Strategies for Building #PersonalBrands.

---

*In this value driven and 'connection economy', skills & talents alone are dime-a-dozen, you need to be able to add value to others and build great connections.*

---

**#PersonalBranding**: The combination of your skills and talents to produce value for others that creates an impression, a perception and reputation becomes your personal brand.

*Succeeding in a #Career and finding a #Job*

*"A resume and cover letter isn't enough anymore and if you're not willing to go the extra mile, the competition will - and you will be caught in the recruitment cycle for much longer than you would anticipate"* ~ Dan Schwabel

**Creating a strong personal brand:**

A. **Ask questions:** You shouldn't be shy to ask or pretend you know everything. Ask for clarification, details, ask for more information. Ask for referrals.  Ask for recommendations.
   *"He who asks is a fool for five minutes, but he who does not ask remains a fool forever"* ~ Chinese Proverb

If you are a job seeker ask yourself these questions:

- I'm I qualified for this job?
- I'm I going to add value to the company?
- Do I have a personal mission statement?
- Does it line up with my personal values?
- Will I be able to work under the conditions stated?
- Will my skills and expertise be utilized to its maximum to benefit the company?
- Where can I find my potential employer?

B. **Be Bold:** Believe in yourself and what you have to offer. You have talents, abilities and skills, both formal and informal. Your confidence can earn you your next deal, or job. One guiding principle I use to launch out confidently into every new venture is a quote by Johann Wolfgang von Goethe. He said; *"Whatever you do, or dream you can, begin it. Boldness has genius and power and magic in it."*You should know the value you add to others. Your uniqueness. You can state this clearly in your personal mission statement. *"Be bold when others are scared."-Thomas J. Powell.*

C. **Clarity**, *Consistency, Constancy*: these are the 3 characteristics of great personal brands; they are collectively called 'the 3C's of branding'.

**Clarity:** Right from the beginning of your career you must be very specific about what you would want to stand for and also about your objectives in life; what you would want to be noted for. Be clear, no ambiguity. Turn your laser focus on that and pursue it with all your heart. This will help you to craft your tagline/slogan out of that. Example: Seth Godin has the slogan; *"Go make something happen".*

**Consistency:** Once you have identified your clear path, you must then stick to it and repeatedly deliver on your word. You say what you mean, mean what you say and do it! This will help you build a great reputation in the market place, thereby establishing your brand. For instance, UT Financial Services (Ghana) still delivers loans in less than 48hours. They have been true to their promise and have constantly been delivering for a decade.

**Constancy:** Having the quality of being faithful and dependable. Now you must position yourself to be seen and heard by your target market; continuously evolving and adapting innovative ways to reach your audience. Pat Flynn calls it "be everywhere", you go to be seen. Coca-Cola has succeeded imprinting its brand on people with their innovative promotional materials and ads. Your goal should be to have a dominant niche.

*Now it's time to* **Create** *or* **Curate** Online:You must create your content to communicate your expertise. You may consider blogging in your field of interest; if you love fashion, blog and talk about that. You should create a portfolio of your expertise; show the public what you have to offer. Produce quality original content and see your brand soar high. Another thing is content curation; if you can't create then curate. Find out where you can have access to all the relevant information in your field of interest then, summarize and share on social media platforms. Example if it's in the area of sports, share latest and most relevant information about particular games. This will enable you establish your authority in that area. Ensure that either whether you create or curate you exhibit the 3 characteristics of a strong brand; *Clarity, Consistency and Constancy in your profiles, CVs and Resume.*

D.  **Discussion Forums:** Join active discussion forums. I am a member of the 48days.net community and it has been very resourceful. You must pick a forum within your niche; don't involve yourself into many things, joining every forum.
*Basic tips for involvement in forums:*
 •   Always read the rules and regulations.

- Choose an appropriate name to use that represents your brand.
- Set your profile right; profile picture and complete bio.
- Be polite.
- Share your expertise.
- Don't spam.
- Ask questions.
- Actively interact with other members of the forum.

There are well resourced discussion forums on Linkedin, Google Plus, Quora and Facebook. Search for the group that not only interests you, but can add value to you. You can post your questions to get meaningful suggestions and answers.

E. **Engage:** Engagement is the key; being on social media requires you to be social. It's not a one way communication; it's two-way. Engage in an ongoing conversation; when you post on Facebook encourage others to comment. You can be asking questions to get your funs and friends interested in the subject.

Tip: Use images and videos to help your engagement with audience on Social media.

They trick is this; *Engagement most often leads to conversion (a purchase), as it provides ways to stay-top-of-mind to your audience.*

Advantages of Engagements:

- It builds trust.
- It provides you ways to get feedback with target audience.
- It builds brand/customer/audience loyalty.

F.  **Free:**Free for my brand?

Let me share a story with you; some time ago a friend of mine (Theresa) contacted me to help promote a young budding musician (KK). I agreed and quickly mapped out a few strategies I could use to help; radio airplay, interviews, events and social media. During that period I was recording one of my Audiobooks, so I thought it wise to use a portion of KK's track for the intro. I got that mixed, created a demo and sent a copy to Theresa, she loved it and said it was great. I uploaded a copy of the demo on my website and asked folks to listen and give me feedbacks, 95% feedbacks were amazing. I felt I could use that as a channel to promote KK's music.

I then had a call form KK who said he has changed his manager and that the new manager will call me so we discuss issues relating to his music. I welcomed that, only to hear that KK was demanding royalties from me for using a portion of his track as an intro for my audiobook. Huh! I guess you should be wondering how this will turn out.

I eventually decided to remove his track from my audiobook before the final production. Now this is the point and lesson; Many young folks are quick to let money (instant gratification) drive them instead of meaning and purpose. I had a good heart to help him, but he was seeking for ways and means to get money instantly (instead of considering the benefits and wealth he could gain from the long term relationship). NB: There is nothing wrong with taking money for one's creative work; it's the approach and mindset we are looking at here.

The young musician had no platform, and instead of looking at leveraging my platform to help promote him, he rather wanted money right from the onset. (Why will I pay an unknown artiste for a track, if I can pay a well-established artiste whose track could promote my work?)

This is it; every musician needs to create a platform or a fan base to push his/her music. If you are new in the system your goal is to get your music to as many people as possible; let me add this "for FREE". This is one of the strategies Cwesi Oteng used; after haven been in the system for a while with other previous albums and tracks, when he released his single "God Dey Bless Me", the track was virtually available for free download. And because it was a great song, it spread like wild-fire; soon it had lots of airplays, it was 'bluetoothed' and 'whatsapped' across every platform you can imagine. This caught the attention of many folks internationally and locally, and now he has received many international awards. Did it cost him to produce such a great music? Yes, a lot and why should he then give it out for free? To build his fan base and a platform which he can capitalize on for monetary value. Now you can only guess the number of request he receives to be on shows and how much money he earns in addition, through all that.

There are thousands of similar examples of folks who gave out their books, videos, music for free and enjoyed huge returns in the long run. Don't try to hoard stuff, spread them around and with well-planned strategies you can monetize your creative works.

Secondly, this is how differently one can take advantage of a situation by offering a service for free with the hope of higher returns later. When a very creative young lady – fashion designer, completed graduate school, her goal was to set up her own fashion clothing line. She didn't have much money since she was unknown in the industry; and how does she get this done? She approached a couple of famous people in the society and told them about the services she renders and that she will be willing to design and sew for them for FREE. Huh! Yes for FREE they just have to provide the material. She approached me with the same story. This is it; these renowned men will show up on TV and attend other great events with the beautiful designs (attires) made by the lady. Folks will eventually ask "who made them?" Then they will refer to her; that is when she will begin making money. In doing this, her work will be seen by many more people and their friends, thereby bringing her more referral business, that's huge market without expensive advertisement. She is spreading her brand, making meaning and money.

You too can leverage what you have with the right mindset and network. Think win-win in all situations.

G. **Google it:** Find it! Yes, simply find out things for yourself. If you are seeking for employment form a specific firm, study more about them; everything about their management, their goods and services which distinguishes them from the others. You do same with companies and people you are looking forward to partner with in future. You must learn the skill of searching for information on the internet. There are vast amounts of data on almost every imaginable subject online. If you seek, you will find them. Google everything.

H. **Help people:** One easy way to build your brand and position yourself as an authority in an area is to help others; offer solutions. If you are on Twitter, Quora, Facebook, etc. and someone posts a question that you have an answer to, be quick to provide a solution. Spend time in forums on subjects you are knowledgeable in and be providing answers to others.

I. **Invest:** Invest in yourself. You must keep developing yourself; find out ways to better your best. If you want to be known as an expert in an area you must be willing to sacrifice, time, energy and money to get all that you can get and all others that you must get on that area. Don't permit complacency to set in. *"The illiterate of the 21st century will not be those who cannot read and write, but those who cannot learn, unlearn, and relearn. " — Alvin Toffler*

**J. Join:** This is one best kept secret to help you and your brand. Join new communities online. Yes. Mostly if you are one of the very first people who tried something out, you have a higher chance of succeeding at it. Let's take the example of those who quickly jumped into Facebook and Pinterest long ago and created accounts; they had the opportunity to test the system and build influence. This may not always be the norm, but it doesn't hurt if you can make time to occasionally test some of these new systems and websites.

**K. Keep*it real*:** Be Authentic! You don't need to try to impress others or win their approval by what you do. Just be yourself and let the real you standout. Don't fake it; no false information on your CV or profiles. [*A friend of mine remarked that on LinkedIn almost everyone is a 'CEO'; quite an interesting observation*]. Whether real or forgery; your work and identity will definitely be found out.

**L. Listen:** Listen to know where the conversations are happening; where likeminded folks meet; where top business people/ entrepreneurs hangout. Listen to hear where you potential clients and employers are. One of my mentors told me that when he is travelling he always ensured he got the Business/executive class in the plane. He remarked; *"That's where the deals happen"*.

*M.* **Mentors:** "Mentors are those who first see greatness in you and believe can walk side by side with you to till you reach your destination. In truth they never see you in them but rather see a unique talent that needs nurturing. They are not supposed to idols or gods to be worshiped. They don't believe in status but talent and space to make errors as part of experience gathering. Anyone who thinks your breakthrough is tied to his/her fame, name and fortune is a master and you are the slave; you will labor to maintain his/her status." ~ Scofray Nana Yaw Yeboah. You will need a coach or a mentor in your chosen field, to aid you along your career path. There will always be someone who has been where you want to be or at least has an idea that will help you. Don't ignore such people; get a coach. Tiger Woods, Oprah Winfrey, Tyler Perry, you name them; all high achievers have great coaches. Get a coach!

*N.* **Network:** This quote really says it all; *"Your Network determines Your Net worth"*. Connect with people, we are in the connection and collaborative economy and your value comes by your association. Join professional networks; It's all about *'whom you know'*.

Networking generally is about creating connection for mutual benefits. We network every day; from our daily commute, transaction at the grocery shop, the bank, events, etc. Anytime you have a conversation with someone, you are networking.

Attending networking events increases your confidence, provides shared knowledge, widens your contact, makes you get access to more valuable connections and limitless opportunities such as your potential client, employer, partner, etc. In building networks keep this classic quote by Zig Ziglar in mind; *"People don't care how much you know until they know how much you care"*

To project your brand and create value for your clients you must **C.A.R.E**.

Be…

**C - Consistent:** Be dependable, always delivering on your promise. Keep high standards.

**A - Authentic:** Be yourself, be original. Use your unique strengths. Instill the attitude of professionalism; handle everything well.

**R - Rewarding:** Honoring them by your service and product: Look out for ways to reward you clients, followers and fans. Give them something to ensure they always come back. Be remarkable.

**E - Excellence**: Pursue excellence, exemplary delivery. This is one keep that will set you apart; pursue excellence, and be the very best. Give them a quality experience that will be indelible in their memories.

*TIPS to consider in Networking*

- Set goals for your networking meetings before you attend them.
- In your interaction with others focus on them and not you; don't be a self-promoter.
- Understand, seek long-term relationship and don't focus on looking for who can be of help to you at the moment.
- Try to give than to receive.
- Connecting with people instead of just transacting business.
- Be generous and don't be desperate.
- Focus on others' strengths, abilities and qualities.

*"Your network is all the people you know; and all the people who know you; and all the people who know them; who they can recommend you and your services to." ~ Business Networking Success book.*

O. **Outlook:** Your outlook here represents the way you present yourself. The question is; does appearance matter? Yes! It really does; everyone consciously or unconsciously judges and make up their mind concerning people by their appearance.

### 5 Inexpensive Ways to Be More Attractive - Projecting your Brand

We are going to use what I call the '**S.W.O.R.D.**' formula.

The sword here signifies your authority, gifts & talents, abilities & skills. Every gifted person needs this sword to fight the challenges of life to succeed and be more attractive. It's nothing complex; basically simple, but a very effective way to be more attractive.

The great Philosopher, Jim Rohn, once stated: *"To attract attractive people, you must be attractive. To attract powerful people, you must be powerful. To attract committed people, you must be committed. Instead of going to work on them, you go to work on yourself. If you become, you can attract."*

Here you are;

> **S - SMILE:** A smile is a language understood by every tribe, culture and country. It lightens up the darkness in every situation. When you

carry a smile always, you become easily approachable, seen as a friendly person who is attractive and simply charming. It costs nothing but its benefits are huge. Never dress without one, Smile. SMILE ~ See My Instant Life Energizer.

**W ~ WORDS:** Words are spirits and they also carry life. Use them well and you will surely gain the admiration of many. Mishandle them and your reputation is ruined. Choose your words wisely. Knowing what to say is as important as how and when to say it. *Speech may be silver, silence golden, but wisdom knows when to use which of the two.* Your words must be seasoned with salt. Have you ever been so attracted to a person just by his wise words and the manner of they are used? Cultivate the power of the right use of words with right speech tone then you will be unstoppable. *"A gentle answer turns away wrath, but a harsh word stirs up anger"- Proverbs 15:1. Don't forget to be using your brand slogan.*

**O ~ ORDER:** Anything sequentially, systematically and perfectly done attracts attention. This calls for discipline, a great deal of time and meticulously working on tasks, goals and your dreams. You must make delivery of excellence your goal in whatever you do; become a person of much distinction. *"Anything worth doing is worth doing right."* — *Hunter S. Thompson*

**R ~ RESPECT:** Anytime you show respect to someone, you honor the person. Having a sword doesn't make you superior to anyone; it's rather a tool to serve. Firstly, you must learn to respect yourself, treat yourself well, and then secondly treat others with honor. You respect their time, their opinions, and their religion and belief system. This is one key that opens doors to you. Go out today to honor others; your parents, the elders, your colleagues and watch favor flowing to your doors. *"I speak to everyone in the same way, whether he is the garbage man or the president of the university."* — *Albert Einstein*

**D ~ DRESS:** Your appearance matters a whole lot. Key phrase; *"Man looks at the outward appearance"*. As much as appearance can be deceptive, on the average it creates the most lasting first impression. You need to dress good, look good and smell good. That in itself boosts your self-confidence. Believe in yourself and what you have. Don't impress, just express the true beauty in you. *"Your appearance,* *attitude, and confidence define you as a person. A professional, well-dressed golfer, like a businessperson, gives the impression that he thinks that the golf course and/or workplace and the people there are important."* — Lorii Myers

Be visually appealing, see yourself as a product, and package yourself for success. This alone can open doors for you or close them behind you. You must choose your cloths carefully, it reflects your brand; sell a positive image about yourself. Dress for the occasion. If you are a job seeker this is one critical area to pay much attention to. Your dressing also reveals your personality, where you have confidence; portray a positive attitude or low self-esteem. If you have your business, depending on the nature of your job you may have a lee way here. However you must put on your best cloths to project yourself and help you work effectively. NB: *"You are addressed the way you are dressed"*. First impression matters. Check your wardrobe now and make the necessary changes.

*P.* **Publish:** One great way to build influence, followers and to be noted as an authority or a brand is by publishing great content. Using Photos, with platforms like Instagram and Pinterest to build your brand/business. Blogging, white papers and also book publishing. Consider publishing an e-book with Amazon kindle to help establish your authority. Your goal should be to share valuable content that will benefit readers, thereby establishing your brand.

*Advantages of Publishing a Book*

- It establishes you as an authority in a subject.
- It positions you as an expert, a 'go-to' person.
- It opens more doors and other business channels for you.
- It provides another stream of income for you.
- It gives you a competitive advantage in business.

*Q.* **Quality:** quality sells. *"Quality means doing it right when no one is looking."* — *Henry Ford.* Provide quality content, services and delivery. Make it a point not to settle for anything less of yourself and of others. Don't cut corners. Gone are the days when companies or people could put up less quality products and with the aid of TV and newspaper advertisement get a whole lot sold without a sense of remorse, but now things are different, buyers are discerning so you can't put anything out there and go scot-free. One negative review from a client can ruin your long earned reputation. An unsatisfied customer can cause you a lot.

***R.*** **Referrals:** Referrals and Recommendation serves as endorsement for you and your brand. One can easily get a job by word of mouth and recommendation from a friend or partner. Ask for recommendations from people who are influential in your field. Ask for others to refer your services and products to members of their circle of influence. We believe things told to us by our friends than strangers as to what to buy, just by word of mouth. Anytime you are recommended for a job it increases your chance of getting another, because it positions you as an expert or someone who does a job well.

*S.* **Serve:** It's all about service to others. Meeting the needs of people. For students and graduates students you can easily build a good reputation and also get a job with ease by volunteering to serve as an intern in the organization you would like to work with. This is one way most young ones fall short; they go with the intention of getting an income, without which they won't serve. Clear that notion from your mind, offer to serve for free. It may cost you some money but consider it as part of your learning and equip yourself. Learn all you can about the job, be dedicated to it. Work extra hours, do excellent work. When you do an excellent work, wouldn't it be easy to ask for employment from your boss or for recommendations from him? Sometimes this process happens automatically because of your quality of delivery and commitment to the work.

*T.* **Technology:** don't leave technology and social media to only the 'tech-savvy' folks. Embrace it in any way you can; that's the future of business and brands. Take not that if you don't change, change will change you. Be adaptable. Learn and practice.

*U.* **USP:** 'Unique Selling Proposition'. You must know the specific thing that sets you apart from the other job seekers, entrepreneurs, businesses. This will be the main reason people will want to employ you or buy from you. Once you get this done, communicate it clearly and confidently in all you do.

*V.* **Video**: learn to use videos to market yourself and your brand. Have you thought of doing a video resume? Doing a video bio of yourself telling the world the services you can offer them, as an employee a business owner or entrepreneur. Think differently; a video is now wave trending and a lot more people are likely to watch a video presentation than just read. Do a video documentary of your works. If you are in the creative industry, the upload videos to YouTube. By doing this you are giving potential clients a real feel of your work. Consider doing a live video broadcast of your service, as a speaker, author, painter, lawyer, etc. You can always offer something to the world; your niche market. Think of doing a Google hangout, live webinars. Use all these tools to leverage and promote your brand.

*Tips:*

- *Start a video blog or create a YouTube channel for your brand. Do something remarkable (crazy).*

- *Produce quality videos with the goal to educate, entertain, and inform not to sell right away.*

- *There's nothing worse than having a good video with poor sound quality.*

- *Consider having a video series on a particular subject in your niche for your brand.*

- *Have video tutorials, sharing your knowledge and your expertise.*

- *Get video endorsement for your products and services for your brand.*

W. **Work it!:** Nothing woks unless you work it; knowing all these tools and technique is not enough you must step out and practice, do it! Building a personal brand is not one-off thing, it's a continuous cycle that needs to be worked on constantly, if not you will fade out from the system soon. The completion is fiercer than before and it's not going to slow down in any way. You must arm yourself to stay relevant and compete. *"The few who do are the envy of the many who only watch."* ~Jim Rohn

X. **'Xtra'**: Go the extra mile in all you do. It's always better to under-promise and over-deliver than to over-promise and eventually under-deliver. Do more than you are paid for. Give offers to people. Anytime you make clients feel you are giving them something more than their money's worth they would always want to come back and even refer others. If you are a job seeker, do more than just dropping and emailing CV's. Practice some of the listed techniques above, be different, and be daring, build a positive self-image to stand out among your peers.

Y. **Your** Profile: Have a professionally crafted profile on social networking sites. That should be able to communicate clearly your brand, values and skills. I always recommend having an account on Twitter, Facebook and Linkedin.

Z. **Zone**: Your zone – your place of bliss, goes beyond you and your brand. In all this you must know your limit and your circle of influence. You are not called to meet the needs of everyone. Not everything will work for you, know the ones you can handle, ignore the ones you can't and forge ahead. Be the best you can ever be. Stay in your zone; where time losses itself into purpose and meaning. Enjoy your work life.

## Tweeting your way to success

1. Have a complete twitter BIO set, use keywords that best describes you and your services.
2. Set your location right.
3. If you have a blog or website, add the correct URL.
4. Change the default 'egg' profile picture; use a professional photo to present you.
5. Follow industrial thought-leaders that you can learn from.
6. Listen in to tweet conversation and engage with others.
7. Follow prospective companies, recruiting companies, potential partners.
8. Participate in an ongoing tweet chat in the area of your interest.
9. Answer questions, help others. Show your expertise in your tweets.
10. Retweet, best way to promote others and be noticed by the people you retweet.
11. Reply to messages. Don't use auto 'DM' Direct Message.
12. Tweet about 70 % on a professional subject then 30% on other things.

13. Tweet valuable information.

14. Follow and follow back. Don't take offense when others don't follow back.

15. Offer promotion and discount to your product and services.

16. Use #hastags sparingly. Don't hashtag every post.

17. Don't use all the 140 character tweet space, leave room for retweet.

# LinkedIn Profiling Success:

1.  Complete your profile on LinkedIn; you should have 100% completed. Do share your educational background and experiences

2.  Use a professional photo as your profile picture. Present your brand well.

3.  Check your headings, Job Title, don't leave it just as this "CEO", be descriptive, CEO, Dreametrix Ltd., IT Training & Publishing Firm.

4.  Join groups that will enhance your skills and where you can also contribute meaningfully.There are many professional groups on LinkedIn, just search for them.

5.  Ask for endorsement and add recommendations of you by others to your profile.

6.  In your profile summary, promote your expertise by telling what you have accomplished, and how others can benefit from your connection.

## Quick and Easy Tips& Thoughts on Branding #SocialMedia

1. Simply do this: forget about the hype and help people. Solve problems.

2. #SocialMedia can get you the attention you want but not the trust you need. You got to build trust.

3. Let's get this straight personal branding is not about personal bragging, tooting your own horn.

4. Talking about branding it's like this *"You either make it happen or let it happen."* You've got to consciously decide, define and do it.

5. In this era where you can be anything you want to be, its very alluring to miss the most important mark in life – fulfillment and meaning. Remember that what you can do may not be necessarily what you are called to do.

6. In this digital age you can buy 'likes" and "followers" but you can't buy influence.

7. In this social media era, it's either you become relevant or be relegated.

8.  Don't just focus on what you are good at focus on what you can be great at, and work towards it. Be the best.

9.  Develop that one quality that defines you and your work and work at it wholeheartedly.

10.  Remember the world revolves around #relationships – master the art.

11. Social Media has amplified voices but unfortunately many are only echoes. Don't fake it! Be yourself, be original.

12. If you don't change, change will change you – be adaptable, especially with technology now.

13. You don't measure your ROI by the number of likes you get on your post or page. It's simply by making sales. #SocialMedia

14. In this era, it is not so much about being in a hurry to switch jobs but taking time to invest in yourself, building your brand. Personal development.

15. Your personal brand must be built on a strong foundation. Foundation of purpose and

authenticity. What are you building on? Or trying to cover up?

16. You must understand that personal branding takes time and effort, you will need to work on your brand daily, refining and defining your brand message and identity.

17. I believe that in this digital age if you forget about being celebrated, 'liked ', 'followed', 'retweeted', going viral, etc. and focus on helping people, solving problems, genuinely being friendly and trust-worthy, you and your brand will impact more people positively.

18. Listen: Find out what's going on in your community, pay attention to the needs of others; when online and someone asks a question and you have the answer don't hesitate to answer or make recommendations where necessary. In listening, you may also get to know where the job and your prospective client or employer may be found.

19. Quick response: Time is of the essence and speed of trust of trust is needed to drive this. Be quick in response to questions asked by your customers, this calls for preparedness, so you don't be in haste. You must know all about

your product (YOU) to talk about and answer questions relating to it at any time.

20. We are in a fast changing global era and you must learn to change or be changed, new technology every day, even some of the tools we use today may be outmoded tomorrow, be open minded and a life-long learner. That should be one of your personal values for your brand – *life-long learner.*

21. Update or be outdated: As you are building your expertise in your chosen filed, make it a must to study the latest resources in that area; news, books and all materials that will keep you on top of the game. This is where many fail. They stick to their old materials, what they used to know and never bother to update.

22. Stay ahead of the game: You must be a step ahead of your competition and your folks, be hungry for information. Ensure that you know your stuff well that even in your dreams when you are called to attend to a need, you can do it 'on the fly'. Master your craft.

## Facebook User Behavior:

**What your attitude may be saying: An Amateur or a Pro**. Your #Brand.

*"There are four ways, and only four ways, in which we have contact with the world. We are evaluated and classified by these four contacts: what we do, how we look, what we say, and how we say it. ~ Dale Carnegie*

1. Amateurs send friend requests to everyone but the Pros are strategic because they believe in this 'your network determines your net worth'

2. Amateurs' display their ignorance openly by their post and comments (they are quick to break the news without getting the facts, spams others) but the Pros are particular about what they share. They create value for others.

3. Amateurs join every group but pros join selective groups that are profitable.(it's not

about the number of groups but the quality offered)

4.  Amateurs tag people in every posts they make and craves for attention but the Pros tag only when relevant.(so they command attention)

5.   Amateurs share lots of their personal photos and tag everyone in every photo (very annoying habit) but the Pros only tag a person only when they are in the picture or to convey specific information.(e.g. Info-graphics)

*"Every pro was once and amateur. Every expert was once a beginner. So dream big. And start now."*

# 7 Sins to Stop Committing on #SocialMedia

1. **Passwords**: Change your password often and follow the rules of secure password creation: minimum of 8 characters, the longer the better, mixed with characters and numbers, upper and lowercases. Ensure that you can remember it. Don't use the same password for all your email addresses and social log ins. *Sharing your password*: this may seem a no-brainer but hey this is where most folks get it wrong. You don't inbox folks your password at any time. There was a viral fun scam on Facebook which asked users to type in their passwords as a comment and that it will only appear as asterisks ********* Huh? Many fell victim to this. Beware!

2. **Private is Private:** Yes, we all have a private life, some personal secrets, and these should be kept as such. The fact that one needs to be genuine and build trust doesn't guarantee sharing everything online. Set boundaries. Posting pictures and talking about the latest gadget you bought, that's not so cool. Keep your private pictures private, unless you are a porn star, even that. Did you know that the photos that most ladies share on Facebook have been used by scammers and hackers on

other sites, duplicate profiles, impersonation and others?

3. **Home Alone:** Very dangerous: when you post or tweet, like "boring day I'm home alone"," feeling lonely" etc. Any such message that reveals nobody is at home but you. It's a sign of inviting robbers and other malicious folks into your house, especially when you have made your location known. Watch out.

4. **Vulgar language:** words are very powerful and one must be conscious of this. This can sometimes be tricky as to what is bad language, but hey the user most of the time knows it. Your tweets, feeds, and post reaches people you may never meet, and guess what? They are forming an opinion about who you are. You may say 'who cares?' but at the end you will know. Choose your words wisely. Insults and curse words are not appropriate. Don't let the idea that you have your 'right of speech and freedom' get you swayed: 'rights' come with responsibility.

5. **Needy**: We all have needs, so don't let the whole world know that. Don't be the one always complaining about something, asking for favors: It's good to ask for help but know

what and how to do that. Another class of folks will quickly ask you to buy their product, sell you something, and ask for money, etc right after you've become friends. Very bad approach. Nobody owes you anything. Stop whining.

6. **Stalking**: you want to follow every celebrity on Twitter, sending friend requests to every "big man", thought-leaders, change makers, on Facebook. What happens here again is if such folks don't get the feedback needed, like a follow back, friendship, favor, etc they move to "bad-mouthing" them. Stop stalking and start beating your own path to success.

7. **Annoying set of things to stop**:
   I. Mass messaging people on Facebook (group message), simply the worst to do.
   II. Tagging people randomly in every post and picture.
   III. Begging for page 'likes' or post 'like' and 'sharing'
   IV. Poking '*like seriously*' what does that suppose to do?
   V. Inviting people to every event, even when they are out of geographical location for a live event.

VI.  Posting your status update or sharing your blog post on the timelines/walls of others.

VII.  Game app requests Spamming: much need not to be said on this. Quit it!

## Dos and Don'ts:  Your Brand Website and Graphics

1.  **Brand and Domain names:**
    Brand Names: Here I have what we call *"The Rule of '3'"* i. You either have one name, examples here: Yahoo, Google, Oprah, Jacquar, Versace. ii. You go for two names or words, check these ones: Tiger Woods, Michael Jackson, Ralph Lauren, Mensah Otabil, Albert Ocran, Agya Koo. iii. Here it's initials or acronyms, example: BBC, CNN, BMW, BKC, R2BEES,
    Domain Names: Yes, as much as possible avoid using very long domain names and names that makes it difficult to remember. Most new entrepreneurs present all their ideas in their domain names.  Simplify, although this is not a

rule of thumb, for best practices it helps. You may break the rule and still succeed. That's the power of a brand.

2.  **Don't use sub-domains:**
    Sometimes, I find it interesting to see so called experts, especially web designers and companies use sub domain extensions as their website names, example: successconference.webs.com, tastytom.webs.com. I say, that unless you are Seth Godin, who has built that credibility and brand all these years to use sethgodin.typepad.com and still drive crazy traffic and loyal readers to his posts, you don't dare that now. My personal recommendation is that you don't use any sub-domain and blogging site's name for your blog. Example: kofiBoakye.blogspot.com, yaafrimpongmaa.wordpress.com. Buy your own domain name for your blog and business site, standout from the crowd. eg. briantracy.com, amaeyawdebrah.com, bernardkelvinclive.com

3.  **Blog it Not:**
    Let's face it blogging is great but the crust of the matter is this blogging is not for everyone, period! There a millions of blogs available now

on the internet, this is not to discourage you from blogging, but to help you align your purpose, perspective and brand well. So the earlier you draw your career development plan and brand objective, the better it will help you choose what platform to use to reach your target audience, to some the best place will be a YouTube channel, others will just be Facebook. Find out where your market is and reach them. Think about this.

4.  **Website images:**
    For best SEO results and brand positioning, I advise its best not to use Googled images from other websites for your logo design or web graphics, it's unprofessional. Standout by virtue of your graphics, make it unique. Moreover these images may be copyrighted.

5.  **Avoid complex logos:**
    Brand identity: your logo represents your brand, so avoid complex logos. NB: *Less is more*. Great brands always have simple logos; take the example of Nike and DHL.  Simple and professionally done, that should be your goal; simplify! Did you know that about 95% of leading brands have only one or two colors for their logo? Example Facebook, Coca-Cola, Whatsapp, McDonalds, BKC, CNN, InCharge

Global, Seloart, Msimps, Vodafone, etc.
#Brands

6.  **Keep your website updated:**
    Outmoded and un-updated websites always
    turn potential clients away and devalues your
    brand. Imaging someone searching for very
    important information only to land on your
    website with outdated information, wrong
    email address, no contact, or invalid telephone
    number.

7.  **Redesign or Modify your site:**
    Make it a goal to have your website design
    modified or totally redesigned at least once
    every two years. Get a fresh look and appeal.
    And avoid using outmoded software.

8.  **Check and validate:**
    Do quality assurance, your site is your online
    storefront and you are selling yourself and
    business, so always crosscheck the content you
    put out there. Let it represent what you stand
    for and truly do for business. Don't fake it.

9.  **Don't just be personal be professional:**
    Personal branding doesn't mean you should do
    everything by you. Hire experts in the various

areas, a copywriter to do your sales pages, proofreader and web developer.

**10. Stop the Flow:**
Don't always jump into the latest band-wagon, latest softwares and apps on the market, find out if its best for your niche and your brand, tried and tested. Don't be like everyone else. The fact that one model works for your competitor doesn't really mean it's going to work for you. Remember your USP.

**11. Go Mobile:**
The internet age is fast moving towards mobile; where more people are accessing the internet using their hand-held devices. So in other not to cut off lots of people from accessing your website, ensure that your site is mobile friendly. Giving uses the ability to surf your site on mobile devices. Also your site must be optimized to load fast. People can't afford to waste time waiting for a page to load, they will rather leave.

**12. Don't Assume:**
Don't assume everyone knows what you know, or even think it' irrelevant to them. Learn to share what you know in simple form. As you build your brand, focus is to inform,

educate, by adding value, do think of all the little things you do as a way of strengthening your brand.

## 13. Try it:

Test things, trial out new stuff, don't just stick to your comfort soon, what you used to do, and how things have worked in times past. Venture new areas; ask yourself the question, how I can do this differently. Think in the box, think outside the box, and think without a box. In that you will be challenging yourself to think outside the box.

*"People aren't really buying your stuff. They are buying a connection to you and your point of view."*

## Tools to Monitor Your Brand Online

Here are the social media tools that will enable you to keep track of your brand and other competitors in your niche.

1. **TalkWalker:** *www.TalkWalker.com*

It helps you: Monitor the Web for interesting new content about your name, brand, competitors, events or any favourite topic with Talkwalker Alerts!

Talk walker alerts are an easy and free alerting service that provides email updates of the latest relevant mentions on the Web directly to your email box or RSS feed reader.

2. **HootSuite**: *www.hootsuite.com*

Hootsuite is a social media management system for businesses and organisations to collaboratively execute campaigns across multiple social networks from.

3. **GoogleAlerts**: *www.google.com/alerts*

Google Alerts are emails sent to you when Google finds new results -- such as web pages, newspaper articles, or blogs -- that match your search term. This is one of the easiest ways to monitor what's been said about you online. You should set alerts for your name.  You can create alerts for latest news on a trending topic, celebrity, brands, etc.

## 4.  **Klout:** *www.Klout.com*

Klout is a website and mobile app that uses social media analyses to rank its users according to online social influence.  You can connect most of your social channels to Klout to help measure your influence across those networks. You can login with Facebook or twitter to sign up. Klout measures influence based on the ability of its users to drive action across the social web.

## 5.  **SocialMention:** *www.SocialMention.com*

Social Mention is a social media search and analysis platform that aggregates user generated content into a single stream of information. It allows you to easily track and measure what people are saying about you, your company, a new product, or any topic across the web's social media landscape in real-time. Social Mention monitors 100+ social media properties directly including: Twitter, Facebook, FriendFeed, YouTube, Digg, Google etc.

## 6. NetVibes: *www.netvibes.com*

Monitor and analyse everything on a single platform with Netvibes. Now, you can eliminate noise and get smarter, more relevant results by combining powerful adaptive analyses with expert human curation.

# Personal Branding Interviews 101

In this section, I share with you stories of young folks (Social Entrepreneurs) who are building brands in various ways as a social change *(The New Revolution)*. Share in their success story and their brand building strategies. They are youth driving positive change; utilizing branding as a service.

## 1. Gideon Commey

Gideon Commey **[GC]**, Bernard Kelvin Clive**[BKC]**

**BKC:** *Let's get to know you personally; tell us a little about you and what you do.*

**GC:** Gideon Commey is an Environmental Activist. He is the Co-Founder and Campaign Strategist of the Ghana Youth Environmental Movement (GYEM). I am passionate about young people and the environment and have spent the last 6 years as a community organizer mobilizing young people for social and environmental campaigns.

**BKC**: *What sets your heart on fire and why are you passionately pursuing this?*

**GC:** The desire to see transformational change happen in my generation sets my heart on fire. I want to be part of change; I want to work for change, I want to create and lead it. I'm passionately pursuing this because I believe in activism. "Activism is about being an active citizen; it is the bills I pay for living on this planet".

**BKC:** *What has been your cardinal principle or philosophy for success?*

**GC:** My cardinal principle or philosophy for success is service. The person who serves people regardless of his position, possession, power, popularity and prosperity is the greatest.

**BKC:** *What has been your experience in using social media as a tool to drive home your passions?*

**GC:** I have used social media to drive change for the past 5years. In activism, we call it 'Clicktivism', meaning click activism. I started off as a community organizer involved in mobilizing lunch and clothing for thousands of underprivileged children in marginalized communities. I used social media for this purpose. Then when I became a full time environmental activist, I have used social media to mobilize hundreds of young people to run successful campaigns against environmental pollution and to fight against climate change.

**BKC:** *Do you consider yourself a brand and why?*

**GC:** Yes, I consider myself a brand because I am original, an innovator and influential figure in my field of work. I'm a leader in my community, I have followers and I stand the test of time.

**BKC:** *Would this knowledge of you unconsciously branding yourself all this while lead to a change in focus on branding yourself now? How do you think this knowledge of the brand you've created impact on your future activities?*

**GC:** No it wouldn't because I have never spent time, resources and efforts branding myself. I believe real branding is about being yourself and being what you want to be. I'm not perfect but I always strive for excellence and that I believe is already a brand. The knowledge of this brand will push me beyond my limits and boundaries. This is because I cannot lower the standards; I can only maintain it or surpass and exceed it. This calls for more knowledge, dedication and sacrifice because perfection is not optional again.

**BKC:** *If you are to choose a phrase, caption or word that will capture all that you've done, what would you want to be known for?*

**GC:** Transformational Leader

**BKC:** *What advantages does creating a 'personal brand' have for the job seekers and entrepreneurs in this age?*

**GC:** Building a personal brand will aid young entrepreneurs to build a community and that is where change begins. It will also make them influential because branding is about character and credibility and people would only follow you when you possess these two. Character and credibility also mean trust and when people trust you, they listen to you. Building a personal brand will also open them to diverse opportunities since everyone wants to be associated with a brand that can stand the test of time

**BKC:** *What will be your billion dollar advice to the world on building personal brands as a tool for social change?*

**GC:** You cannot build a brand without providing a service. So brand building is about serving people. Service is everything. Any brand that stands the test of time and is immortalized eventually was grounded on the foundation, principle and philosophy of service.

## 2. Regina Agyare

Regina Agyare**[RA]**, Bernard Kelvin Clive**[BKC]**

**BKC:** *Let's get to know you personally; tell us a little about you and what you do.*

**RA:** I am a Ghanaian woman who is proud of her heritage. I come from a family of supportive parents and siblings. I have a curious mind and an adventurous spirit. I am a software developer and a social entrepreneur, who is passionate about technology and social change.

**BKC**: *What sets your heart on fire and why are you passionately pursuing this?*

**RA:** I want to fuel economic growth in Ghana by providing technological solutions to SME's to help them grow their business. I also want to use mass technology to drive human potential.

**BKC:** *What has been your cardinal principle or philosophy for success?*

**RA:** Never Give up

**BKC:** *What has been your experience in using social media as a tool to drive home your passions?*

**RA:** For me social media has transformed my business and brought opportunities that I could have never imagined was possible. As a startup, my marketing budget was low so I relied solely on Social media to promote my business. I am able to get business, referrals and my work is featured online in different international and local news articles. From social media I was able to get people to buy into my vision of using technology to bring social change and they lent their support by contributing in diverse ways to make it a success.

**BKC:** *Do you consider yourself a brand and why?*

**RA:** I am definitely a brand because people associate me with technology and social change. I am an expert in the usage of mass technology to drive human potential and I have the credentials together with a track record to support that claim. I am also associated with quality service and prompt delivery. These qualities define brand Regina Agyare and as my brand grows, so does my reach and impact.

**BKC:** *Would this knowledge of you unconsciously branding yourself all this while lead to a change in focus on branding yourself now? How do you think this knowledge of the brand you've created impact on your future activities?*

**RA:** I think strategically of everything I do because I believe in keeping my brand fresh and alive. Since business is about relationships, having a good brand allows me to attract new opportunities and allows me to get recommendations. It also helps me get the needed support in my social work in communities.

**BKC:** *If you are to choose a phrase, caption or word that will capture all that you've done, what would you want to be known for?*

**RA:** Regina Agyare – Social Change through Technology

**BKC:** *What advantages does creating a 'personal brand' have for the job seekers and entrepreneurs in this age?*

**RA:** Quite frankly without a personal brand you will fail to stand out as a job seeker and entrepreneur in this age. With it you can get more opportunities and carve a niche for yourself that will ensure your success in any endeavor you pursue.

**BKC:** *What will be your billion dollar advice to the world on building personal brands as a tool for social change?*

**RA:** Think carefully about how you want to brand yourself and make sure all you do goes to build that brand.

## 3. David AsareAsiamah

David AsareAisamah**[DAA]**, Bernard Kelvin Clive**[BKC]**

**[BKC]** *Let's get to know you personally, tell us a little about you and what you do?*

**[DAA] I am the** founder of the Agro Mindset Organization and Agro Mindset Farm. I guide the Agro Mindset Fraternity with a switch on strategic vision, values, and fresh approach to engaging the youth in agriculture. I have empowered and I continue to empower a new generation of Ghana's youth to take advantage of the numerous opportunities that agriculture presents Ghana to transform them. I am super-passionate about this transformation and I am actively in the front line, doing it and showing others how it is done. I am committed to working on the Agro-Mindset vision so as to help lift Ghana's agrarian economy to prominence and by so doing, champion the cause of a new 'green revolution' which involves getting people to practice their knowledge in agriculture to satisfy industry gaps and requirements.

**[BKC]** *What sets your heart on fire and why are you passionately pursuing this?*

**[DAA]** What keeps me awake is the generally low interest in agriculture among the young generation, especially in their ambition to pursue careers in this sector; posing a threat to the sustainability of the agricultural industry over a long term. Notwithstanding the fact that agriculture could remain a primary sector for the youth, it suffers from an image problem. There is a lack of provision of good training and the creation of the right image to pique and maintain young peoples' interests in agriculture in many countries in the sub-Saharan region, of which Ghana is no exception. The Ghanaian society in general has a negative perception towards agriculture. Creating the right image and interest is much more important now than ever, given that food security, as well as its equitable economic transformation, depends on sustained agriculture. If farming, agricultural research and extension services are no longer seen as a viable professional future for the younger generation, then "who will grow the crops that will feed the world"? This aggravates me and sets my heart on fire.

**[BKC]** *What has been your cardinal principle or philosophy for your success?*

**[DAA]** Falling in love with what I do. Although this has become a mantra for motivational speakers, the moment your passion becomes your career, you have to face realities and stop chasing fantasies. I have organized my life, my resources and time around my passion which is anything to do with agriculture, in development and business sense. Surrounding myself with the right people gives me a higher leverage to get fired up all the time.

**[BKC]** *What has been your experience in using social media as a tool to drive home your passions; your success story?*

**[DAA]** I don't think people should build a career in social media because we can all manage contents on it. What matters is how to deliver to your customer with an intention of creating value. Social media is a very useful tool created with the intention to help make new alliances and connect with old allies. Overtime, this is drifting as almost everyone uses social media for personal branding. People I have never met know me now and I even consult for a lot more. Much awareness is created for our program and the organization.   98% of the people who encourage me found on social media.

**[BKC]** *Do you consider yourself a brand and why?*

**[DAA]** Agro Mindset could be well-thought-out as a brand. I define a brand as an impression of a product or a service that an organization provides. Branding is seen as the marketing of an impression or image so that more and more people recognize it and become aware of that brand. I go to cash money in banks and when it's ready, I am called to receive it by the name "agro-mindset". People see me around and call me by agromindset, even at home. It is gradually becoming a common name on the lips of people around me. As at now, anyone sees anything agricultural or have any query on agriculture and relays it to us for a solution or tags us through the social media. For example, I was there one afternoon when I received a call from HaygrovePolytunnels (http://haygrove.co.uk/) to come to Ledbury to meet their Boss. To end that meeting, I had to provide some consultation for them. Two months later, they are doing feasibility studies of a potential market for Ghana's 70% smallholder farmers. I want a future where our brand easily comes to mind when people think of agriculture.

**[BKC]** *Would this knowledge of you unconsciously branding yourself all this while lead to a change in focus on branding yourself now? How do you think this knowledge of the brand you've created impact on your future activities?*

**[DAA]** As at now, any subsidiary group that emerges from the 'Agro Mindset' concept bears and will bear the mother name. There have been times that I thought of changing the name but since we are a determined group with a paradigm that is poised to see Africa's agricultural mindset revamped to reflect a new generation of leaders pioneering agriculture in Ghana and Africa, it would be good to maintain that self-explanatory name. Our focus is not to promote poverty stricken farmers who feel that farming is just to work on a piece of land for subsistence but rather to raise up business-oriented farmers of plural inclusion in Africa as a whole, beginning with Ghana.

Looking into the future, we aim to evolve to become a world class pan-African education provider to educate Africa's new cohorts of entrepreneurial-minded agriculturalists; enlightening within our students the critical reasoning and problem solving skills and sparking within them, the interest to take up the vast opportunities present in agrarian African countries. Regarding youth and agriculture, it goes without saying that the stakeholders are expected to involve the youth in innovation and policy formulation. Not much is said about what the youth can do themselves to facilitate their involvement in these processes. We are keen about this transformation and will forever be actively in the front lines leading by example. Our brand will assist us in diverse ways to set up a University that would lead the development of teaching and research in agriculture, agri-business, food, and land and property management that explores the nexus between the different fields of knowledge.

**[BKC]** *If you are to choose a phrase, caption or word that will capture all that you've done, what would you be known for?*

**[DAA]** David Asare Asiamah – I would want to be known for 'agromindset'.

**[BKC]** *What are some of the advantages that creating a 'personal brand' has for the job seekers and entrepreneurs in this age?*

**[DAA]** A personal brand arouses an expressive emotional reaction in another person around about what an enterprise represents and its abilities. It could quicken networking and assistance that will come your way when people trust you.

**[BKC]** *What will be your billion dollar advice to the world on building personal brands as a tool for social change?*

**[DAA]** It is good to build a brand that people can easily associate with but if there is a slip-up or failure, it becomes indelible too and people will associate your brand with the blunder and not the proper things you have done. In that situation, you will thirst after another breakthrough moment to evoke a good name but it might be too late. We all must protect our brand with integrity and lasting good leadership skills.

## 4. Raindolf Owusu

Raindolf Owusu[RA], Bernard Kelvin Clive [BKC]

**[BKC]***Let's get to know you personally, tell us a little about you and what you do?*

**[RO]** My name is Raindolf Owusu, 22, a final year student at Methodist University College Ghana studying Information Technology. I am the founder of Oasis WebSoft, an IT start-up. A software development company that aims to solve Africa's problems using software technology and also our mission is to build infrastructure that will ensure that the West African sub-region is not left behind in the continuous evolution of information technology. My software and web projects include deploying Africa's first web browser called Anansi web Browser, a linux distribution called Anansi operating system targeted at education and AnansiCalcpad, African Grading program and Dr Diabetes a web application that allows you to know your diabetes status online.

**[BKC]***What sets your heart on fire? Why are you passionately pursuing this?*

**[RO]** I believe that the way forward for advancement in technology is the collaborative use of open source technologies. Africa is on the move, and software and technologies are powerful tools for boosting economic growth and poverty reduction.

**[BKC]***What has been your cardinal principle or philosophy for success?*

**[RO]** Staying focused and keeping my eyes on the bigger prize.

**[BKC]***What has been your experience in using social media as a tool to drive home your passions? Your success story.*

After I successfully launched and started operations at Oasis Websoft, I did not have any financial assistance to help me advertise our work through the main stream media so I decided to use social media eg. Facebook , twitter and blogs to talk about my work. We have grown a large following online , who continuously  support our work and share my updates with their family and friends. Today thousands of people read our blog , visit our website and recommend our works to many people in Africa and beyond.

**[BKC]** *Do you consider yourself a brand and why?*

**[RO]** I don't consider myself a brand but just the founder and driving force behind my company. Oasis WebSoft is the brand most people know and have utilized some of our great works online, on their phones or anywhere else.

**[BKC]***Would this knowledge of you unconsciously branding yourself all this while lead to a change in focus on branding yourself now? How do you think this knowledge of the brand you've created impact on your future activities?*

**[RO]** Branding came as a perk with my work at Oasis WebSoft and I always have joy in my heart when I receive emails from people telling me my story inspires them. It's a great thing to put yourself in a good position for people to see you as a brand. This brand has created a lot of opportunities for me and my company. It's easy for people to know we are a genuine company by simply googling my name or company's name and that's a game changer for us.

**[BKC]***If you are to choose a phrase, caption, word, that will capture all that your very essence, what would you be known for?*

**[RO]**Raindolf Owusu – The African Hacker

**[BKC]***What advantage(s) does creating a 'personal brand' present to the job seekers and entrepreneurs in this age?*

**[RO]** It opens a lot of doors for you since you have spear headed a lot of great things despite all the challenges in Africa. Don't just talk the talk, walk the talk☺.

**[BKC]***What will be your billion dollar advice to the world on building personal brands as a tool for social change?*

**[RO]** Continue to stay true to your beliefs, to always be yourself and to be proud of your accomplishments.

## 5. Miranda Agnes Quainoo

Miranda Agnes Quainoo [MAQ], Bernard Kelvin Clive [BKC]

**BKC:** *Let's get to know you personally, tell us a little about you and what you do?*

**MAQ:** My name is Miranda Agnes Quainoo and am 23 years old .A fourth year student of The Ghana Institute of Journalism. I am the project Cordinator of Greight foundation-Ghana. Greight is an international NGO which empowers, educates and mentors young girls from difficult backgrounds; girls and women empowerment is at the heart of this foundation's activities. I founded 'pass-a-book-on' two years ago (an organisation that spreads literacy among children).This initiative has touched the lives of thousands of children in Ghana. I love working with and for deprived children and the disabled. I mentor children at the Akropong school for the blind (that is one of my most honouring experiences).I am also associated with Share Your Lunch and a number of NGOs' and social initiatives. I dream of becoming a bilingual journalist and a best-selling author.

**BKC:** *What sets your heart on fire? Why are you passionately pursuing this?*

**MAQ:** The fear and burden that people's life will not get better if I don't feel responsible enough to do something to touch their lives. My passion gives my life great value and I can't imagine having a better life outside what I do and enjoy-making a difference.

**BKC:** *What has been your cardinal principle or philosophy for success? Share your challenges and success story.*

**MAQ:** Whenever God puts a dream in my heart; it could be a project in a deprived community, I can't rest till I have made it happen. It is all I think about. No matter the odds and the limitations and discouragement, I go through with it. Sometimes, I tone the dream down but I never completely push it away. I believe EVERYTHING is possible. EVERYTHING!I procrastinate a lot (I am working on it though) .That's is the Goliath I have to slay completely.

**BKC:** *What has been your experience in using social media as a tool to drive home your passions?*

**MAQ:** Surprisingly effective. I have never doubted the power of social media and media as a whole but my work is so much easier using social media. I reach out to masses about a project within a short time and I usually get the fairly good response. I have networked with organisations and people doing similar things and even got some donations through social media.

**BKC:** *Do you consider yourself a brand and why?*

**MAQ:**I have never actually thought of myself as a brand. It is more about the organisations I work with and for. Branding the projects and the initiatives has been more of the focus. So considering that, I would say yes. This is because I feel that we are at a place where we can be known for one thing or the other. When people think of 'pass-a-book-on' they relate it with literacy. If I have branded myself, then I must have done it unconsciously.

**BKC:** *Would this knowledge of you unconsciously branding yourself all this while lead to a change in focus on branding yourself now? How do you think this knowledge of the brand you've created impact on your future activities?*

**MAQ:** Yes, definitely. I am certainly going to make an effort to do that. I think our volunteers and donors will be more willing to invest into future initiatives if they know they are associating themselves with a credible brand.

**BKC:** *If you are to choose a phrase, caption or word that will capture all that you've done, what would you want to be known for.*

**MAQ:** Making a difference by being different.

**BKC:** *To job seekers and entrepreneurs of this age, what do you think are some of the advantages they can capitalize on by creating a brand?*

**MAQ:** Personally, I think branding is like an aroma, something that attracts people to you. Before they actually taste the real meal, they must experience the aroma first. And we all know that bad aroma will repel. Personal branding does half, if not all of the job for the job seekers and entrepreneurs.

**BKC:** *What will be your billion dollar advice to the world on building personal brands as a tool for social change?*

**MAQ:** Branding is everything; it is your uniqueness. It basically separates the jewels from the stones. You have to be known for something and it is absolutely great that you can be known for something you choose to be known for. If you work towards it, you can give the exact impression you want to give about what you do. People always want to associate themselves with good traits; like integrity, quality and excellence. So in your work as a person seeking social change, you will need to deliberately and consciously create, build and sustain your personal brand.

## 6. Emmanuel Ansah Amprofi

Emmanuel Ansah Amprofi**[EAA]**, Bernard Kelvin Clive**[BKC]**

**BKC:** *Let's get to know you personally, tell us a little about you and what you do?*

**EAA:** A social entrepreneur, Business executive, a youth advocate and Speaker. Founded Africa Youth Network, a youth developmental NGO and runs Stages Multimedia & tours, a vibrant multimedia & tourism company head quartered in Accra.

**BKC:** *What sets your heart on fire? Why are you passionately pursuing this?*

**EAA:** Passion to make a change that inspires, leads and share a smile with people especially children and youth.

**BKC:** *What has been the cardinal principle or philosophy for your success?*

**EAA:** Faith and Values, Leadership by example.

**BKC:** *What has been your experience in using social media as a tool to drive home your passions?*

**EAA:** Very intriguing and innovative. Have been able to run many programs and touched many lives through social media.

**BKC:** *Do you consider yourself a brand and why?*

**EAA:** Yes, because you are what you see yourself to be and people or organizations will see you in the same way.

**BKC:** *Would this knowledge of you unconsciously branding yourself all this while lead to a change in focus on branding yourself now? How do you think this knowledge of the brand you've created impact on your future activities?*

**EAA:** Branding helps you keep you in check and focus. You've got to always improve and aim to be the best in your field.

**BKC:** *If you are to choose a phrase, caption or word that will capture all that you've done, what would you be known for?*

**EAA:** Lead and Inspire Change /Man-on-a-Mission.

**BKC:** *What are some of the advantages inherent in creating a 'personal brand', that job seekers and entrepreneurs in this age can make use of?*

**EAA:** It's your brand that will make or unmake you because people buy the brand more than persona. Just as they say we are what we eat.

**BKC:** *What will be your billion dollar advice to the world on building personal brands as a tool for social change?*

**EAA:** Lit the passion in you to make the change you want to see. If we are to make this nation or Africa better it must start from the grassroots and the grassroots includes you.

## 7. Randy Osae Bediako

Randy Osae Bediako [ROB], Bernard Kelvin Clive [BKC]

**BKC:** *Let's get to know you personally, tell us a little about you and what you do?*

**ROB:** Randy Osae Bediako is a young vision-minded Ghanaian-based entrepreneur. Randy believes that he belongs to a new breed of entrepreneurs whose motivation for going into business is not primarily to satisfy a need and get rewarded for it, but most importantly to use business as a tool to advance the kingdom of God on earth.

He refers to himself as a *'spiritpreneur'*, a term he coined from two main words –Spiritual and entrepreneur – meaning one whose business has a direct or indirect positive impact on God's kingdom.

As founder and CEO of Kharis Media Ltd, Randy oversees a growing indigenous print media business empire with eight sub business units which would eventually evolve into full-fledged companies under the Kharis Group.

Kharis Media Ltd. is popularly known for its flagship product; Ghana's award winning BEST Christian magazine, Kharis Magazine.

In barely two years of existence, KML is providing direct and indirect employment to over 30 individuals.

Randy has proven to be a phenomenal business brain regarded as a young dynamic emerging corporate leader. His indignation towards the plight of the needy in society has motivated him to establish the Kharis Foundation, a charitable department which offers aid to underprivileged individuals in society.

Randy holds a bachelor's degree in Agricultural Science from Kwame Nkrumah University of Science and Technology, Kumasi, and is married to Lois Osae Bediako, a legal practitioner by profession.

**BKC**: *What sets your heart on fire? Why are you passionately pursuing this?*

**ROB:**I am extremely passionate about the media. The media over the years has proven to be the most effective tool for mass communication.

I believe my mandate is to build strong businesses in every sector of the media in order to gain mastery over the dissemination of relevant information for the total benefit and transformation of humanity.

**BKC:** *What has been your cardinal principle or philosophy for success?*

**ROB:** *'Impact or Die'* is one of my own self-inspired, success-driven catch phrases for focus. This three worded phrase has proven to be my cardinal principle for success.

This principle connotes that success is not an option but a necessity for survival.

**BKC:** *What has been your experience in using social media as a tool to drive home your passion?*

**ROB:** Without any contention or argument the social media platform has been an extremely effective global communication, branding and advertising outlet for me and my organization.

**BKC:** *Do you consider yourself a brand and why?*

**ROB:** Most definitely, I am a brand. We are all brands whether we are conscious of it or not. The mere fact that I occupy some space in another person's mind automatically makes me a 'BRAND'.

**BKC***: Would this knowledge of you unconsciously branding yourself all this while lead to a change in focus on branding yourself now? How do you think this knowledge of the brand you've created impact on your future activities?*

**ROB:** Soren Kierkegaard, a Danish philosopher and theologian, once said "Life can only be understood backwards, but it must be lived forwards".

It is obviously impossible to go back into the past and change people's perceptions about you, but at the same time there is a great opportunity now to create new perceptions about yourself that will make others perceive you in a brighter light.

**BKC:** *If you are to choose a phrase, caption or word that will capture all that you've done, what would you be crave to be known for?*

**ROB:For Now:**

Randy Osae Bediako- synonymous with "**Kharis Magazine**" (BEST Christian Magazine in Ghana).

In the future as the Entire Vision Unfolds;

Randy Osae Bediako - an altruistic Christian Media Mogul.

**BKC:** *What are some of the advantages of creating a 'personal brand' for the job seekers and entrepreneurs in this age?*

**ROB:** For the job seeker, personal branding helps communicate a clearly distinguishing message about who they are and what they can offer to their potential employer. For the entrepreneur (employer), branding helps your target audience to know your unique strengths, skills, passions and values.

**BKC:** *What will be your billion dollar advice to the world on building personal brands as a tool for social change?*

**ROB**: Never has it been easier to affect change through the power of personal branding than now. In today's competitive job market until you think of yourself as a brand you cannot survive.

Remember, people do not just buy products and services; they buy into people and for that matter personal branding is inevitable in the course of social change.

Understand that when people believe in who you are and what you have to offer, only then do they accept your ideals and practice them.

# Resources and Links

*Here are some of the great places and great minds I have been learning from, experts in their various fields: Books, Bloggers, Speakers, Podcasters, Professionals, Individuals making a difference with their brands and business.*

1. www.copyblogger.com
2. www.48days.net
3. www.socialmediaexaminer.com
4. www.sethgodin.com
5. www.chrisbrogan.com
6. www.MichaelHyatt.com
7. www.DaveRamsey.com
8. www.PersonalBrandingBlog.com
9. www.entrepreneuronfire.com
10. www.MitchJoel.com
11. www.ExpertsAcademy.com
12. www.JohnMaxwell.com
13. www.PatFlynn.me
14. www.RobinSharma.com

### Books

15. Tim Ferriss Books (The 4-Hour) Series
16. Think and Grow Rich – Napoleon Hill
17. 48 Days to The Work You Love – Dan Miller
18. Platform – Michael Hyatt
19. Tribe – Seth God

# Conclusion

*In conclusion…*

## Choose to be Outstanding:

The hard truth is this: the world is full of followers, people waiting to jump into the next big thing. Many are afraid to take the plunge, to lead, to live their dreams, to be different; nevertheless many are ready to rally around something they believe in, after a takeoff. To create and lead your niche, do this: don't try to stand out among the crowd, you build the crowd, you take the lead by building a community of like-minded individuals, with your own style and strategy. Focus on a worthy cause in your society, something you support, you advocate for.

At this point the major question for you is this, what can you do differently?

*"Here's to the crazy ones. The misfits. The rebels. The troublemakers. The round pegs in the square holes. The ones who see things differently. They're not fond of rules. And they have no respect for the status quo. You can quote them, disagree with them, glorify or vilify them. About the only thing you can't do is ignore them. Because they change things. They push the human*

*race forward. And while some may see them as the crazy ones, we see genius. Because the people who are crazy enough to think they can change the world, are the ones who do." ~ Apple Inc.*

Pause with me here, David Raymond Quojo Asiamah, Randy Osae Bediako, Benjamin Gregory Aggrey, Gbenga Edison, Raindolf Owusu, Kwame Pocho, Nana Ama Yeboah Diamond, Gideon Marcel Commey, Kobby Blay, Kwaku Sonny, Maximus Amertorgoh, Kane Mani., Regina Agyare… What do they have in common? These are not the known faces on TV or print media, these are ordinary folks who have identified their talents, added skills and are impacting societies, communities in their own way, thereby building a niche brand of value. These ones are driving a social change, a movement in various ways. David, is transforming the face of Agriculture in Ghana, whetting the interest of more young people to venture into Agro farming; Randy, is transforming the face of magazines(print Media) in Ghana, one can hardly talk about quality Christian magazine and print house without referring to Kharis Media; Benjamin, is passionately empowering African Women through 'Woman2.1 Summit' yearly, there is no single force like that, you can't talk about women empowerment driven by a youth without referring to Woman2.1 Summit; Gbenga, is using technology to drive the Agro industry in Ghana like never before; Nana Ama and Kobby, are using Social media as a tool to educate people on health related issues through their online and offline activities with Sangy Nursing Services and GhanaHealthNest respectively; Pocho, young and passionately using his talent/hobby to give new face to photography in Ghana, telling the youth that they can make money from their passions if they learn how to take stunning pictures Pocho. Rhyme Sonny, has rebirthed the spoken word and poetry in Ghana with series of social activities and events through the innovative group POETS. Maximus Ametorgoh, Kane Mani and Regina Agyare are using technology to educate the ordinary man on the street, developing mobile apps for innovative use for SMEs. (*Tech is the new ish*). Gideon Commey from Ghana is building an environmental activist community, as a way to support the social well-being of the people in his country – preserving the environment. He has followers, he becomes the leader. His brand shines aside doing social good. Here is the catch, all of the names listed didn't really start out to build a global brand but to pursue a worthy cause, to help humanity, and service is the key. *Personal Brands with Passion and Purpose; solving People's Problems.* If they are doing it, you too can also do it! You can excel in your career! Let's do it!!!

Go, Make it Happen!

## About the Author

Bernard Kelvin Clive ~ *CEO of BKC Consulting,* Amazon Bestselling Author, Speaker, with the passion *to inspire others to live their God-given dreams and enjoy their daily lives. ~"Inspiring and empowering souls"*

He is known to simplify complex ideas into tools that inspire people through his speaking engagements, books and training. He contributes regularly to *Young Men's Perspective Magazine*, *Today Magazine*, *Ewatch Magazine*, and *Hero Magazine*. He is also a columnist for ModernGhana.com. He also blogs at his official website BKC.name.

Bernard is set apart from his peers by a strong social brand and his simplified yet thought-provoking message. He has helped hundreds of people self-publish their books through training and workshops, and has inspired thousands more to live their dreams. His motto is, *"Inspiring and empowering souls one text at a time."*

Bernard is also a blogger and member of the 48days.net online community. His article "Dig Another Well – Dream Another Dream" was featured article of the week in July 2010 at 48days.net.

## Public Speaking

Bernard has delivered motivational speeches across the country to diverse audiences from junior high schools to universities, churches to corporate boardrooms. He has a passion for inspiring and empowering people to live their dreams and enjoy life, no matter what their age or background may be. He was the guest Motivational Speaker to deliver the commencement speech at the 46th congregation of the College of Art and Social Science at the Kwame Nkrumah University of Science and Technology.

## Radio and Television

Bernard also hosts Youth Wise Forum on Top Radio 103.1 FM every Saturday morning at 9AM. Bernard has been a regular guest on many of Ghana's radio and TV talk shows, including, ViaSat 1, ETV, GTV, and Metro TV. He is also the first international guest author to be featured and interviewed on OurWishRadio.com and *'Own Your Dreams with Ona Brown'* broadcasted on LOVE860.

## Online Media and Software

Currently Bernard has three motivational apps for mobile devices: Inspiration Kitchen 101, Just a Minute, and the Bernard Kelvin Clive inspiration app. He also co-created the online digital assistance tool ElectronicPA. Bernard is host of a daily inspirational podcast, which listeners can download for free from iTunes. Currently his podcast is the leading title in the Self-Help category.

## Social Entrepreneur/ Voluntary work

Bernard has served as a team member for various NGOs and associations, as well as pioneered many startups and events. He is president of the Motivational Speakers Network (MSNgh) and co-founder of Dreametrix Limited, a company that organizes motivational seminars, webinars and training for companies, schools, churches, and mentoring sections for students at MSNgh. Dreamertrix also offers IT Consultancy services, web site development, domain name registration and social media marketing. Bernard serves as Assistant Director for the Africa Youth Economic Forum (AYEF). He is also the founding member of other organizations including Author Heritage, the Ghana Start-up Capital Fund, MADEit Investment, His Royal Ambassadors Network, and Official of Model African Union Summit 2012.

## Education

Bernard graduated from Kwame Nkrumah University Science and Technology (KNUST) with a Bachelor of Arts degree in Integrated Rural Art and Industry. He earned a Postgraduate diploma in Management Information Systems (MIS) from the Ghana Institute of Management and Public Administration (GIMPA). He also has a certificate in Graphic Design, and has undergone training in Information Systems, Product Designing and Packaging, and the 3D Modeling Programme Rhinoceros 3D, under world-renowned Industrial Designers Glenn Lewis (North Carolina State University, US), Frank Arthur (US), and Mark Kwami (US). Old Student of Ofori Panin Secondary School(OPASS).

## Stay connected

www.BKC.name
www.twitter.com/bernardkelvin
www.facebook.com/bernardkelvin
www.youtube.com/bernardkelvin
www.rebelmouse.com/bernardkelvin
www.pinterest.com/bernardkelvin
www/linkedin.com/in/bernardkelvin
http://www.amazon.com/author/bernardkelvin

*Tel:* +233244961121
*Email:* info@BKC.name

## Books by the same author

1. *The Art of Personal Branding*
2. *Your Dreams Will Not Die*
3. *Inspirational Kitchen – Discover 30 Ingredients to Spice up your Life*
4. *Just A Minute – 52 Seconds: Simplified Motivation – Words to Inspire*
5. *The Writers' Dream: How to Write, Publish and Sell your Book Successfully(Paper Back)*
6. *16 secrets I Learnt From My EX*
7. *How to Publish and Sell your Books with Little or No Money*
8. *Do Not Die with your Music Unsung*
9. *EnjoyLife360 ~ Simple Secrets to a Happier Fulfilling Life!*
10. *How To DO It At Any Age*
11. *The No Nonsense Guide to Effective Time Management: 187 Little Tips that Create Big Impact*

*If you really love this book, do recommend it. Thank you!*

One more thing, I would be glad if you can take a minute to write a kind review on amazon for me.